Beyond That Further Hill

Beyond That Further Hill

by **Macdonald Carey**

University of South Carolina

Many of these poems have appeared in the
New York Quarterly.

Library of Congress Cataloging-in-Publication Data

Carey, Macdonald.
  Beyond that further hill.

  I. Title.
PS3553.A6688B48   1989   811'.54   88-36266
ISBN 0-87249-621-X (pbk.)

Dedicated to

Father Jerome Vereb C.P.

CONTENTS

FOREWORD

I was no more than 9 years old when I took a bus from Rye to Port Chester to go to the Capitol Theatre to see a 1942 war movie called *Wake Island* with Brian Donlevy, William Bendix, Robert Preston, and Macdonald Carey. I remember it was an exciting film about American troops trying to hold a Pacific base against overwhelming odds—*Newsweek* called it "Hollywood's first intelligent, honest and completely successful attempt to dramatize the deeds of an American fighting force on a fighting front."

Some 44 years later in 1986, I was editor of the *New York Quarterly* poetry magazine, and reading upwards of 50,000 poem submissions a year. I had trained myself to read fast and judge surely, because most of the work that came in the mails was middling to awful—either competent trained-seal stuff, or else flat pancake non-poems, or else a lot of maudlin magpie noise. Read fast, stuff the things back into their self-addressed return envelopes. But I remember once I came across a poem submission that was immediately exciting—clear strong voice poetry—genial and sharp images and a magnanimous heartfelt line. It was by someone named Macdonald Carey. I remember thinking to myself: this couldn't be that same Macdonald Carey who made *Wake Island* way back in 1942? But as I read through more of the poem submission, I saw that some of the poems were about the Hollywood studio system back in those 1940s. My God, I thought, it *is* the same Macdonald Carey! And his writing is every bit as exciting and honest and powerful as his acting! My eyes fell on these lines, from "A Further Tyrone Power Chronicle":

> The studio sent him out to be
> Seen with a starlet every night
> Twentieth had 10 male stars and
> 10 female stars
> They tried to cross breed them socially
> Ty, Cesar Romero, Don Ameche, Etc
> And Linda Darnell, Gene Tierney, Etc
> They got as many different duets
> Out of those 20 as mathematics would allow

Well we go ahead and publish this Tyrone Power poem, and some other poems also, including "My First Review," "If It Ain't Broke Don't Fix It," "Parable," "A Papal Visit," and "Round and Round She Goes," in the next few issues of *NYQ*. And pretty soon I begin hearing from other people all over the country, about what great poems they are. Charles Bukowski phones me long distance from San Pedro, California, to ask me who the hell is this Macdonald Carey? He writes great stuff, Bukowski says, really great stuff. And I think to myself, that's pretty high praise coming from Bukowski who has a pretty acid opinion about 99% of what passes as contemporary poesy. And later, when Buk gets Macdonald Carey's manuscript for this book *Beyond That Further Hill*, he writes me the following on 8–12–88:

> On Macdonald Carey's book manu, I just read half of poems, phoned him, told him I need read no further, delightful read, he had his paragraph. I will read remainder at my own pelican pleasure. I just wish more writers knew how to play the line like Mac does,

there's very little to read in the world. A fellow like that just naturally adds a couple of years to your life because no matter what happens it will never be quite as dark as it was.

High praise indeed, and now I know I will have to dig deep to see if I can figure out how Macdonald Carey has achieved this extraordinary poetry. To be sure, he has a singular voice—its straightforward genial manner rings with honesty and irony and equanimity. And he also has a beguiling ordinariness to his writing so he seems to be someone we've known all our lives; and his plain style diction and simple sharp images reinforce that sense of total trustworthiness in the artist, in the man.

At times Macdonald Carey's voice is so ingenuous he takes us in with its modesty and self-mockery—as in these lines from "Just Let Us Make One Diagnosis":

Supreme bliss! My name was seventeen down in
Sunday's crossword puzzle and more people
Have mentioned that than have ever commented
On my acting or anything I've ever written or done

But behind the ingenuousness of his voice there is a deeper authentic artistry at work. The voice in these poems usually leads us through anecdote after anecdote, story after story, all of them seemingly unrelated to one another. And it's precisely this loose structure of the anecdotal style that achieves the brilliant effects; Macdonald Carey has trained himself to yield absolutely to the purest stream of consciousness flow of his poetry, very much like the moment-to-moment life of an actor onstage. Most of the anecdotal stories are like zen *koans*, paradoxical and cryptic riddles that seem to sum up whole lifetimes of karma experience.

Sometimes these anecdotes bunch together to form associational clusters, a harlequin collage of quick sketch self-portraits that invariably arrive at an aesthetic configuration that is true art, intuitively right.

In fact, Macdonald Carey's voice is so assured and insouciant, you hardly notice when he goes into some casual and astonishing cluster figure system. Consider, for example, these lines from "The Girl":

We are both awkward strangers at the party
But
She makes it look easy
Greets gargoyles, converses with druids
Stoned to the gills in milky ways
Oh the stars are out tonight stumbling over each other

Or consider the economy of the sudden shifts of voice in these nine lines from "Parable", in which Carey describes a wrap party following the completion of a motion picture:

The first drink some big hulk of a grip
Comes over and tells me
What a great guy I am
To work with
The second drink
He begins hitting me on the
Shoulder—half joking—half serious
Third drink
He calls me a stuck up actor bastard

Or as a technical exercise, let the reader try to figure out exactly how the following lines from "(Untitled)" evoke such purity of pathos and completely unsentimental innocence:

I am a boy again on Jackson Street in Sioux City
A boy of ten

I watch the car hit my dog
I run to the dog and yell at
The car which speeds on its way
I yell for someone to help me
Someone to help my dog
But no one helps me
No one comes
He dies there as I hold him
I dream this dream to this day too
Sometimes I'm the boy and sometimes I'm the dog
And sometimes I am both

I suspect Macdonald Carey's extraordinary success as a poet has something to do with Macdonald Carey's extraordinary success as an actor. There is the same innate sense of stage presence, and the same infallible instinct for timing. There is also the same modesty underlying his finest performances on film—in that early war movie *Wake Island*, or playing the F. Scott Fitzgerald character in the 1949 Paramount film of *The Great Gatsby*, or for 23 years introducing his daily soap opera, "Days of Our Lives" with the same words, "This is Macdonald Carey . . ." Macdonald Carey is endearing as an actor because he seems to be so relaxed, so natural; he never seems to be "acting", because he is always being himself. One of his colleagues, the late Henry Fonda, said it in a 1986 interview:

> I very quickly realized there was a difference between watching an actor you knew was acting and watching somebody who made you forget he was an actor. I began thinking, That's the way I want to be. Please, God, don't let them see the wheels go around, don't let the machinery show. Whatever I do

in preparation is to make it as natural and real as possible.

Henry Fonda's prayer is the prayer of all serious artists in any form of expression—"*Please, God, don't let them see the wheels go around, don't let the machinery show.*" Well, I did a Craft Interview with Macdonald Carey that will appear in issue #36 of the *New York Quarterly,* and I can tell you that in that interview Macdonald Carey reveals that he knows all about the wheels and the machinery of both acting and writing. He is enormously articulate about the technical side of acting and writing, but his artistry is that he does not let that technical side show, when he is at work. He *seems* to be so easy, so relaxed and natural, and he has allowed his own voice to embody an entire lifetime of experience without letting us see the wheels go around, without letting any of the machinery show.

And it's an enormously rich and varied life that Macdonald Carey's work embodies: as a young child in Iowa; as a boarding school student at Exeter, New Hampshire; as a college student at Wisconsin and Iowa; doing graduate work at Iowa. Then on to his early radio work, on almost all the network soaps, on "Stella Dallas", "The First Nighter", "Theatre Guild of the Air." His stage work, in which he ran through almost the entire canon of Shakespeare's plays, both in Iowa and later at the Globe Theatre in Texas; on Broadway 1940–41 in "Lady in the Dark" with Gertrude Lawrence, and in 1953–54 in "Anniversary Waltz" with Kitty Carlisle. In his film work, the 1947 *Dream Girl,* based on the Elmer Rice play, with Betty Hutton and Walter Abel; the 1949 *Great Gatsby* Paramount film with Alan Ladd and Betty Field and Barry Sullivan and Howard da Silva; the 1949 *The Lawless* Paramount film with Gail Russell and John Hoyt; the 1949 *Streets of Laredo* Paramount film with William Holden, William Bendix and Mona Freeman; and the 1961 *The Damned* Columbia film with Viveca Lindfors, Alexander Knox and Oliver Reed. And as we mentioned, on television, from the early days of "Doctor Christian" and the other soaps, to his 23 years on the NBC daytime program, "Days of Our Lives".

In addition to his public identity, Macdonald Carey has lived an intensive private life—as First Lieutenant in the Marines, as family man, as practising Catholic and Minister of the Eucharist, as recovered alcoholic, as poet—and all of these different identities interweave through the pages of the poems of this book.

"Beyond That Further Hill"—and beyond that straightforward genial voice, and beyond all the brilliant word play and quick diction shifts and figure systems, and beyond the zen anecdotal free flow stream of consciousness—beyond all that, there is a deeper subtext of symbolist acceptance of things as they are. Macdonald Carey says it himself, in these lines from "Round and Round She Goes":

> When you get to be my age
> There isn't much of your interior territory
> You haven't explored
> There are few trips you can take
> Without stumbling over a familiar landscape

I think it's that sense of familiarity that Macdonald Carey feels with his own interior territory, that makes it so easy for any reader to feel equally familiar with the materials that are presented in these poems. Yet one also senses a fibre toughness, and a perservering spirit:

"Il faut souffrir pour etre belle"

How curious this world is—my being that 9-year-old boy going to see *Wake Island,* feels now like it's no more than a poetic anecdote; and my sitting here in my Manhattan apartment typing out this foreword to Macdonald Carey's collection of poetry, feels like it's just another anecdote. I suppose in some way these two anecdotal happenings are related, in some weird stream of consciousness way. I'm beginning to feel like someone in a Macdonald Carey poem.

William Packard

New York
1988

FOREWORD

I first came across the work of Macdonald Carey in the pages of the *New York Quarterly.* I was taken at once by the ease and humor and warmth of the writing. Here was feeling that was not afraid of feeling, here was feeling that was not afraid to laugh at itself.

Yet these were but a few poems. Most poets can be good once or twice or maybe once more but not too many hold up over the long course.

Upon reading these, I am happy to report that Macdonald Carey has. And you will soon realize this too.

That Mac has spent almost an entire lifetime as a Hollywood actor and yet is still able to write these delicious poems, well, that's quite some miracle. Hollywood is the killer of souls. How this man ever retained his sensibilities and probably even enhanced them is beyond me.

But welcome, anyhow, to this Daring Old Man on the Flying Trapeze.

To this wonderful and original show.

Charles Bukowski

December 12, 1988

Beyond That Further Hill

My First Review

That summer I caught up with school
After spending a semester shipping out on a
    steel freighter

We never made it around the world (just half
    way around the U.S.
From New York to San Francisco
Via Panama Canal).
I had a semester to make up.

I rented a room on the University of
    Iowa Campus
From a Rhodes Scholar and his wife
The man was finishing up his Doctorate
They had a 4 year old boy who was brilliant
And precocious and obnoxious.
The boy was being brought up
By the gospel according to Spock and little else.
He was allowed to do anything he wanted
And was encouraged to speak his mind
Even when not preoccupied with the classics
(Like the learned Lipsius he knew Latin
    & Greek).

The locks were taken off all the doors in
    the house
And I couldn't take a bath in privacy.

The boy would wait all day and come in
    the bathroom
And sail his boats between my legs in the tub.
I finally blocked the door with a chair so he
    couldn't get in.

The next day he wouldn't leave his sandbox.
He spent all morning in the sand pile
Chanting to himself under his breath.

He's declining verbs his Mother says.
His Father and I stake out
In the neighbor's yard
To overhear him.
He is saying the same thing over and
    over again.
"Mac Carey is a son of a bitch."
"Mac Carey is a son of a bitch."

Horace

I'm coming home after an endless day at
    the studio.
I was in the beginning, middle and the end
    of the script.
I entered first and exited last. Six A.M. to
    seven P.M. and I get up at four.
As usual it was the times between the
    beginning and the middle and the end
That sucked my blood and sapped my juices.
I drive Sunset and go to Fountain to finesse
    the traffic,
Cut back to Sunset on La Cienega and coast
    home to Benedict.
I compliment myself on my cunning and
    comfort myself
With the green shade of the tress on
    Lexington and the thought
There is no nagging wife or chattering
    children to grapple with at home.
I am wrapped in total euphoria as I drive up
    to the house and get out of my car.

A giant German Shepherd sits in front of my
    front door.
We stare at each other.
I walk past 40 doors and gates guarded by
    dogs snarling at me.

3

The Hound of the Baskervilles—its jaws
        dripping saliva and blood
And Cerberus his fifty heads grinning at me.
But suddenly the German Shepherd gets to
        its feet, stretches and wags its tail
Welcoming yet reproving me for being late.
I read the dog tag on his neck. His name is
        Horace and he lives in Holmby Hills.

He has a phone number.
I call it and a machine answers. So I leave my
address and the message I have Horace in
        my charge.
Horace is hungry and I give him a can of
        Kal Kan,
Provender left from my dead
        bloodhound's provisions.

Some of my bloodhound's (he's been gone
        five years),
Some spoor must remain to have drawn this
        dog to my
Doorstep, drawn him to this least safe house
        on a
Traffic choked street where there's a
        car totaled
Every year for twelve years. A bloodhound's
        spoor is only
Matched by the lion's whose dung is so
        insufferable it

Is purchased to frighten deer and coyotes and
    raccoons away.
Mine is the only house in the neighborhood
    free from
Intruding wildlife.

But something else is at work here. Horace and
I understand this and we understand each
    other.
He shuns the kitchen and walks into the
    library and
Sits down in front of the poetry—the
    classical section.
He doesn't move till the front door bell rings.
It is the dog's owner.

Horace rises, walks out the door and into
    a vast
Cadillac in my driveway.
The owner thanks me and as he drives away
    I see
Horace sitting bolt upright on the back seat
Every inch the major poet.

The Good Samaritan

Father Lopez admits
He steals when necessary.
His homily Sunday was the story
Of his Filipino Father
Who let a drunken marine
Who'd been in a fight
Sleep it off on his front parlor couch
And sent him off the next morning
With carfare to his base.
A homily on charity.

I told the good Father of my four days liberty
In Manila in World War II.
I am the youngest lieutenant in our group.
We have flown in from Mindoro.
Since I rank lowest I am sent off
To find a bottle of booze while others
Will wait for me at the apartment
Of a Miss Concepcion.

They are still fighting outside Manila
And there is a sudden blackout.
I head for the last light that went out
And knock on a door in the darkness.
I am admitted and asked my name and I say
I am from California, from Los Angeles,
From Hollywood, I had worked at Paramount

And yes I know their son,
Charlie Gomorra who is a makeup man
For Wally Westmore and plays the ape
In all the Dorothy Lamour movies.

We spend the night talking.
The next day and the next night.
Then it is Easter morning and I go to mass
With the whole family and sit in the
        choir loft
Looking down on a sea of mantillas.
It is the Filipino women. All their men
Are off fighting the war and they
Fill the church with black lace and faith
        and hope.

I tell this to Father Lopez and ask him
Not to tell the story till I do.
He says he can't promise me anything
And reminds me that plagiarism is stealing
From one writer and research
Is stealing from several.

Christmas Season

The Christmas season began early this year
With the theft of the traffic mirror,
The one I put up across the street to warn of
    southbound speeders.
It ends on Christmas Day when the mirror
    reflecting northbound
Speeders
Is smashed by a brick.
The week before Christmas I work every day.
Monday I am rehearsing in my dressing room
    when I get a message
From the office.
It is urgent I call a Ralph Parker in
    Lawton, Oklahoma.
He says it is urgent. He has moved heaven
    and earth to reach me.
I call him and Ralph Parker answers, "Your
    cousin Ed Clark just died.
Mrs. Parker and I been takin' care of Ed for
    years and he just
Up and died. We want to get back our mobile
    home. But Doctor Pike,
Ed's foot doctor, has got himself appointed
    executor and tied up the
Estate."
I don't know any Ed Clark I say, I don't
    remember any Ed Clark who's
A cousin.

"Well Ed used to talk about his cousin
        Macdonald Carey on
Days of Our Lives and how old Mac's old
        enough to be dead but
There he is still playin' that doctor on
        television. You must
Know Ed, he's worth 40 million and owns
        part of Wyoming, Mississippi
And Oklahoma.
His grandmother's name was Mahoney."
"Of course!" My memory suddenly comes
        alive. "I remember I had a
Grandmother named Mahoney."
Ralph says get a lawyer and hurry down
        here. Pike's got the
Estate and there's a million in cash in the
        checking account and
A million coming in every month from oil
        leases. I'm scared Pike'll
Get his hands on it—and he hangs up.
Well I call up my son Steve who's a lawyer
        in L.A.
He gets a lawyer friend of his in Oklahoma
        City (a Spradling) to take
The case.
And that takes care of Monday.

Tuesday I have a message at the studio to
        call Spradling.

I do and Spradling says he has talked to
    Ralph that morning
And Ralph hung up on him after saying he
    had his .38 out and
Was leaving
To blow Pike's brains out.
So we get to Mrs. Parker on a three way
    phone connection
And she says today's been a teary day. "I
    been here tryin'
To get to the beauty parlor—weepin' in
    my rollers.
I can't do nothin' with Ralph and Pike's
    made a pass at me.
We can't get a lawyer to get our trailer
    because all the lawyers in
Town are busy with divorce cases."
Spradling says tell one of the lawyers it's Ed
    Clark and 40 million.
He'll put your case on the top of the stack.
Mrs. Parker says she will and to call Mr. Lamb
Who's a friend of Ralph's. Now we call Lamb.
Lamb says he discovered the body three days
    ago with Ralph.
He was so excited he knocked over one of the
    piles of
Crisp one thousand dollar bills stacked beside
    Ed's body which was
Lying in the living room of his mansion
    which has crystal chandeliers

In every room—but no plumbing—because
    old Ed hated
Water. Presumably because as an oil man
    he'd drilled
So many dry holes where he hit water not
    oil. Home is
Where the heart is.

Anyway Wednesday comes around and we
    talk to Ralph again.
He has called to warn us Pike's lawyer is a
    man called "Cock."
Ralph's lawyer's name is Schwartzer.
Meanwhile we have discovered Ed Clark's
    mother and
My grandmother are sisters by the name of
    Mahoney and Grandfather
Carey who sold groceries to Ulysses S. Grant
    and Abraham Lincoln
Married one Julia Anastasia Mahoney in 1873
    in Galena, Illinois.
The other Mahoney girl married a Mr. Clark
    who moved south.

Thursday Ralph Parker calls again to say he
    went to Ed Clark's
Funeral
"First time I ever let myself get near a
    Catholic church

I sat in the back row.
Still don't understand them rites."

Friday Spradling calls and says a second
      cousin showed
Up in Dallas who's closer kin and rightfully
      claims the estate.
Christmas comes and New Years.

January 2nd Ralph Parker gets his
      mobile home.
I get peace
Though it is very dangerous getting in and
      out of my driveway
With both mirrors gone

If It Ain't Broke Don't Fix It

A guy I knows publicity agent
Just gave a party
Celebrating the dedication of his star
On Hollywood Boulevard.
The fact no one came to the party was
	headlined by the Times.
Publicity is a doubtful Aladdin's lamp to rely on.
I once did an awful movie with Shelly
	Winters called
"South Sea Sinner" where the Times reviewer
Panned me. Wendell Corey was
Awful he said. My publicity agent called the
Times and demanded a retraction. I got one—
The Times reviewer published a long
	piece apologizing
To Wendell Corey for having mistaken
	Macdonald Carey
For him.

Old Tom

"Depend on it sir,
when a man knows he's to be hung in
 a fortnight
it concentrates his mind wonderfully."
                                    Samuel Johnson

It is Sunday and
I just saw Old Tom again.
He's 94 and he lies in his room
With the shades drawn waiting to die.
Sometimes he gets up when I come to
    see him,
But mostly he lies in bed and lets me draw
    the shade up
While I give him communion.

He keeps asking me to take more of his trees.
Most of his trees are gone now,
Given away to friends and strangers.
But I say, "Not today Tom, I haven't the
    time today."

He has some kind of Old World reverence for me
Because I give him communion and he insists
    on kissing my hand.
I always protest but I let him.
Then I pull the shade down again and go.

Is it we're all partners now in waiting?
I no longer mind you kiss my hand at all.
But for that
The room is empty of us both.

I put off moving the trees
Though now's the time for planting.
As if the putting off
Could put off anything.
For that we hold
Hands now.

Vigil

The moment just before I go to bed
    gets shorter
Every year
The moment just before I turn out the light
    and record
The position of the bed from where I stand
My hand upon the switch

I started the habit of photographing
The room in my mind
Just before I turned out the light
To make me feel at home in strange rooms
In strange or foreign places and to find
    my way

Or if there were a lamp beside the bed
I'd make sure where
The door was before I switched it off

But now I just turn out the light and
    don't check
Anything at all
As if I know the dream I'll have will bring
    me to
Other doors and other rooms
And other light.

Santana

The Santa Ana winds have come and
The world is clean again.
An old black and white movie changed
    to color
Half way through and everything come alive.
Even the Oleanders don't look dirty anymore.
The Standard station signs are bright blue
    and white and red
And billboards are slashes of color bordering
    the streets.
Yellow black and brown and green and purple.
Even the drab of the old Whiskey A-Go-Go
Building has richness.

A redhead walks down the sidewalk taking
Sips from a brown paper bag.
She keeps turning her head to the left
As if to brush something off her shoulder
    with her chin
Or see something in the buildings she
    is passing.
Or is she trying to turn her face from the
    bright sun?
A man in a grey uniform is walking behind her
Brushing things off the sidewalk into
    the gutter
Which blow right back on it.

It is a windy day.
"A day to make you restless," I say to a girl
    in the elevator.
"A day to put you on your toes," she says.
I drive home after work and pine needles are
    in rows along the street
Beneath their trees windswept clean.

Really not the day for birds to let their young
Fly free from the nest.
But as a man said to me today
"If I didn't have horns I'd spread my wings."

The winds have been in my garden.
Umbrellas are inverted toadstools among the
    figs and roses
I swim a path through the cream of leaves
    that covers the pool
And dive for sunken furniture and
    children's toys.

Henry Brachman

Poor Henry Brachman died. I was on
My way to see him with some fresh fruit,
    the one
Thing that seemed to spark his interest
    last week
When I saw him. Gave it to old Tom
    instead whom
I intercepted on his way to the
    Jordanian family
Which lives nearby. Eleven people in a
2 bedroom house in Northridge. The matriarch
Of the family is threatened by death too—
    an aneurism
Which will reach her brain any day. Tom is
Giving them grape vines and a fig tree.
He is dying too and would have walked the
    two blocks
To their house if I hadn't shown up.
    The Jordanian
Lady brings him food wrapped in grape
    leaves she
Has been borrowing from him. Soon they
    will have
Their own vines. It was hard to leave.
The Jordanian lady wanted to cook dinner
    for us
There on the spot. Tom tells me Lois admired a

Dress she was wearing last week and she
    tried to
Take it off then and there and give it to
    her. They
Receive death threats regularly—strangers in a
White white neighborhood. Not white as in
The milk of human kindness. They stand out
Red and warm as blood on the cross.
The mass is not sacrificed on the altar alone
And Tom cantankerous as he is—how
    he shines

Among his trees—his beauties as he calls them.
He's still giving them away to live as part of
Him when he goes. I must get the quotation
I got from him—garbled as it was
Something like "The followers of the dream will
Be as worthy as the dream." That's not quite
Right—but there's truth all around it.

But between yesterday and tomorrow
I think of the gift of fruit I was carrying
To a man already dead
When my car stalled at the mental sanitarium
Where people are kept from the world.
Foothill Health and Rehabilitation Center
    it's called.

My car stalled and I phoned my service to get

The message Henry Brachman was dead and
As easily as shifting a shoulder bag
From one shoulder to another

I took that gift to Tom another dying man
Who is giving his fig trees and grapevines
His gift of fruit
To those who will live after him
So that he may live on.

This morning at mass
Msgr. Healy gave me Mrs. Sharpe to visit
At St. Vincent's Hospital.
Is she terminal too?
There is no end to this, I guess.

I'm turning on the computer.

Growing

My boys are all 6'4"
And into their own lives now
We don't see each other much any more
I remember
We had a problem with one of them
He stammered
I kept trying to talk him out of it
(Speech is important to an actor)

The Doctor said "your voice is very
Threatening to an eight-year old. Tell him
You don't mean to sound that way."

I told him about my being an actor and all
And he never stammered again

One night after that
We were wrestling in the living room
After dinner
And I let him toss me over his shoulder

"There," he said
"I threw the whole father."

We Are Each the Dog

Inhabitants of the deserted town which
    surrounds us here
We are each the dog that will not die
But walks the streets past doors and rooms
We pant and tread a vectored path to a goal
    we never see
Our track the sidewalk curb from block
    to block
Through a town with no outskirts

If we'd look we'd see a cat run up a naked tree
And down again. There are no leaves to hide in
The leaves are in two piles and a child makes
    it one pile
And takes it away. The cat goes too

But we are the dog that cannot die and we
    walk on and do not stop
We are the dog that won't look around and
    walk with purpose
Straight ahead
We are each the dog that will not die and we
    walk on and on.

Liberation Theology

Someone brought his
Stuffed dog
To church today

I asked the monsignor what
Church policy was in these matters

He said

As long has he doesn't
Bark or bite

A Night at the Opera

When I asked the cab driver in
Mexico City why he speeded up when
He came to intersections, he said
"Señor that's where the accidents are."

The Chicken or the Egg?
The Egg, of Course

After many a summer
"He succumbed to the temptation to
Use his aesthetic judgment, he corrupted
The purity of commercial dealings
With artistic considerations."
He looked down from the height
Of his ambitions' ladder
And actually saw the-fly-over-people
Eye to eye.
He got dizzy in his inner ear
And it was then it was that it was
Hard to hear
Anything of meaning anymore
Just the sound of the gnawing of
The worm in the apple in the barrel floating
Over Niagara Falls.
All a tumble intact into a safety net
Of taffeta and lace. The antimacassar on
The chair which is his coffin loaded
        with chotchkas
To the point there is no room for him
The ideas have gone out of these
Things he tried to take along.
The automobiles, The TV's, the bomb,
The food stamps and the dildos
Possessed by his possessions he loses face

And headless, footloose and vacuum packed,
    winds up
Spaced out
Pure spirit sealed in a time capsule
Holding nothing but
The assimilated breath of every immigrant
To Los Angeles up to and including 1985
A man for every year is he
Who runs out of tracks in an old locomotive
Churning its wheels in desert sand
Burned out
A Cinderfella
Eating up the time that's left
Chewing carp entrails
A simian facsimile
Spitting out the crumbs of hours
Crawling backwards on time's shore
Into the reptile's egg
To primeval ooze and
A Darwinian dawn
"Boulversé como las golondrinas
En la primavera"
Fowled up

The Girl

Suddenly
I meet her
We are both awkward strangers at the party
But
She makes it look easy
Greets gargoyles, converses with druids
Stoned to the gills in milky ways
Oh the stars are out tonight stumbling over
      each other
While she dances as if she's skiing
Bends in her dress to skirt the snow
I can see it, hear it rustle as I look down at us
From above the air. No one knows we exist.

I knew a solemn girl who drove a
      Thunderbird painted tapioca and coated
In fur and feathers. A fuzzy car.
Not her she drives a black
And red suppository up hills and down daily
Gaily yet not smiling either.
She sleeps curled up in a coil of garden hose
On my back porch all sleek and curvy animal
      in a silver cocoon
Or on a beach whose sand slops over the edge
Into an hourglass double-timed by a
      digital clock
Whose toes and fingers are being manicured—
      a thankless

Job when no hands or feet are showing. Are
    they buried in the sand?

Black caviar, blini and butter are mixed up
In her yellow hair which catches in my throat
    and as
She dives off the gangplank I am
    treading water
Holding out my arms to catch her
And she slips through my arms to the
    bottom of
The blue pool my home is surrounded by
And I never find her again
Except in lenses of
Telescopes and binoculars or
In frosted windows

I felt exactly like this once before.
I am in Spain doing a movie long after the
    Civil War
Having a for me dazzling luncheon as an
    invited extra man
At the home of the banker who had
    staked Franco.
One of Franco's daughters is at the table.
After lunch we pile ourselves into Ferraris
    and Daimlers
And race up to El Valle de los Caidos
That huge Cathedral carved out of
    mountain limestone

Both tomb and monument for the fallen
Of both sides during the Civil War.
The place is closed to the public for us
And we enter the limestone cavern
And one of the luncheon party sits down
At the great organ and plays jazz

Tonight I am an extra man again in Los
        Angeles for a dinner party at
The bistro
But first right now we are at the County
        Art Museum
The "A Day in the Country" Exhibit
Is being closed to the public for two hours for
        our group
The heads of museum are giving a party a
        private showing
We park on the museum grounds and are
        searching vainly
For the private entrance. A legless girl in
        a wheelchair
Is in the parking lot. "Can I help you?"
        She says

How It Feels to Grow Old

How does it feel to grow old?
I don't know.
I guess it makes you
More aware of when you're wasting your time
Or maybe just more aware
And just a little choosier about how you
    spend it
Time that is
Money and food and cars and clothes
And lots of other things
Don't mean as much but this moment
Here
Now
That's the ticket
That's it

But now I've said this
I realize I'm just as fond of
Yesterday
And as for tomorrow—
I can't say a word against it
It's all of them that count
All of them that matter
Yesterday, today and tomorrow
Each and every one is important
Did I say all of them matter?

That's how it feels to grow old.

Library Card

I just found a memo to myself here on
      my desk.
"Get me a new library card for Anna to use."
Anna is 90 and alone living in an apartment
      with my ex-wife
With no friends in this city.

My parents
Every time I'd agree to take an enema would
Reward me with an Oz book when I was
      a child.
And as I grew up I continued to reward
      myself in life with books
For every extra effort on my part.
It is surprising how worthy of reward you
      can find yourself.
My library now exceeds unreasonably
      my history
And the health of my mental state
And long ago outreached my pocket book.
Yet it is a crazy extension of me, not like the
      shell on
A turtle but a kind of tasty and edible roof
      and walls
That house me in a forest of doubt
Where the children and characters that live in me
Can sustain themselves forever

And

I'm going to the library tomorrow.

Pacific

I just found
The picture of
Me standing in the
Jungle in the Pacific
In 1943.

Our squadron mostly
Sat out the war
Moving from island to island
The only
Thing I remember clearly
From three years
In the Marine Corps

Is the rat
That woke me
Every night
On Espiritu Santo

He wouldn't come
Out till I was
Asleep
And I'd hear him
In the dark

Waiting for me

To turn on the light
And see him
Sitting by the empty
Rat trap
Looking at me

The only bait
He ever took from
The trap I'd set
Every evening for him
Was a lifesaver
He never touched
Cheese

I never caught him
And I never saw him die
He still
Comes out at night
And looks at me

Listening

I never sat down and wrote this before.
    I never
Knew how to say it—ever. But I guess I
    never tried
Before either.
But nothing—there is nothing to stop me
    now. No excuse,
Nothing between us now but time, not even
    regret. Time's
Rubbed that out. Time's rubbed out shame.
I never told you I loved you dad. And even if
    I'd said
The words, which I didn't, I wouldn't have
    convinced you.

The last look I saw on your face after you
    had opened
My door in the hotel at LaJolla to
    say goodnight.
I had broken my leg after too many
    breakfast martinis
And my squadron was leaving for overseas
    the next week.
You opened the door and almost hit the girl
    who was
Hiding behind it.

I've forgotten many things about you but not
    that look.
That look on your face. That last look. It
    wasn't shock.
It wasn't disbelief. It was just a look
    of acceptance
Of finality.

But there are other things I haven't forgotten too.
The careful way you carved roast beef during
    the only
Moments of silence at the table that
Held mother, the twins, grandfather
    and always
A guest and me—when you'd ask me if I
Wanted the fairy toast. I always got it because
I was the oldest boy.
Just another way you tried to make me feel
Wanted since I felt the twins, my
    younger brothers,
Had taken my place in the nest.

After we'd eaten we'd all talk at once till
You'd quiet us somehow and say,
"Nobody ever listens to me"
But some part of us was always listening.
I kept listening even though I was way too
Grown up for them by then—listening when
    you told

The same dumb fairy tales to the twins.
They must have traveled deep into me
Because the first night I was in Ireland
    staying in
The Yeats suite at the Old Conna Inn
I took a walk in the evening mist and I swear
I saw the fairies.

And you fed me more than roast beef and
    fairy tales.
You fed me books. My reward after any
    sickness or spanking
Was always a book. I read Mark Twain,
Stevenson, The Rover Boys, The Motion
    Picture Boys, Tom Swift,
The Oz Books, The Horatio Alger Books,
    Detective Stories,
Weird Tales, Dickens, Thackery, Edgar Allan Poe
And Captain Billy's Whiz Bang.

And you let me fill my room with all the smells
In the world. Before I collected stamps
    I collected
Chipmunk and squirrel skins and rocks and
    marbles and
Cigar bands. I remember Mother saying,
    "Charley, that's
Too much. You are a banker, you know."
    That was

When you'd come home at night with a
    cigar band
For me you'd picked up in the gutter on
    5th Street
In front of the Pierce Building where you had
    your office.

You never came to Minnesota with us in the
Summer though you'd sent us there.
    You stayed
Home in Sioux City and worked through
    the summer
So we could go. Just as you'd stayed
    home from
College though you'd won a scholarship.
    You'd turned
The money over to your sisters so they
    could go.

You died that first year I was overseas
And I never told you I loved you
And that I listened to you

Loved you and listened to you.
Listened to you.

Listened to you.

The Latitude and Longitude of Heaven

It only seems the wells run dry
No one yet's run short of tears
Inspiration's block no cause to cry
Don't blame your state on years

Youth is no longer wasted on the young
The young aren't older every day
Implant, transplant behaviour modify
Ripen, ageless with instant replay

The air forever holds the song
The image of the goal's the simple way
Faith eternally relative
But still to God we pray

How careful we must be to prime the pump
With water from the clearest spring
Though what comes out first is red from rust
The waiting's worth what faith will bring
It would be good to bring a cup
Your hands won't hold the stream
That gushes forth once it's begun
It overflows the dream

Books to UCLA

I am donating my books to UCLA but they
    need indexing
Lois was doing the job but gave it up. She
    is taking
A course in thought transference and has ESP
    and a
Very psychic nature. As she went through
    the different authors she'd
Get these vibes just from handling the books.
    She got through
Beckett and Bellows and Burroughs
    with difficulty
Managed Durrell and Faulkner but when
    she hit
Gide she got ill. Graham Greene revived
    her but
Hemingway and Huxley did her in. She quit
    in the face of
Isherwood. Strange, there is a story if not a
    poem here
The aura of the printed word reaches through
    the cover of the book
So the books at Alexandria burned. Big deal.
    Who died?
Here in my own room in my own home on
    my own time

At 10 o'clock at night I am as free as any man
    can be
It is too late for most people to call and I have
    no lines
To learn for tomorrow
Every selfish bone in my body rejoices and
    loneliness is antichrist
Each aesthete, hermit, medieval monk and
    solitary had it all
When they had books and were alone
    with them
So the books at Alexandria burned. Big deal.
    Who died?
I'll tell you who or who they tried to kill
The 10 million generations the first sovereign
    emperor of China dreamed
When he burned all books not dealing with
Agriculture, medicine or prognostication
The 6 million Jews almighty Hitler feared
When he first burned the books in Berlin
So the books at Alexandria burned. Big deal.
    Who died?
Not them they are around me now
The phoenix is alive and well. And so am I.

That Further Hill

Around the corner of my eye
I see
The space a door makes
Before it shuts

At the bottom of my day
I live in that

Narrow place
Between my dream and waking

Near you in the silence when the noise stops

As near you as horizon

And reach for a stone that
Drops
In water

Fish through my fingers

Dust between my toes

There is so little time for waiting
Even the flowers grow behind my back
I don't know when I stopped looking at myself
In the mirror

But I stopped long ago
And not from fear of what I'd see there
It's just I do not want to know
There is always time for that
And now

I know without looking

The Awareness of Maturity

It's not just the grass is always greener
But it would be nice in this world—just once
To be the most popular
Person at my own party
The most admired and envied guest

But the parties I give in my mind
Are so high-toned, the women so
    beautiful—the men
So brilliant in speech and demeanor
That I can't crash them myself

And as for heaven—forget it
I'll never even
Make it into hell

The Art of Seeing

Aldous Huxley was my favorite author for a
    long time
And for an odd reason
It wasn't that I envied him his prose style, it
    was that
He too had trouble seeing without glasses and
We both took the same eye training course in
    Los Angeles.
He got a book out of it and I got in the
    Marine Corps.
But at least I got the eyes put back in
    my head.
The idea was to let nature heal itself and to
Look at the world as a dog looks at it
    with one's
Whole self—in the dog's case with
His nose and in my case with my mind.
The first lesson is easy
Try it just close your eyes and breathe deeply
    and slowly
One, inhale, two, exhale
Inhale, exhale
One, two
One, two one, two
You've let your eyes close, you're breathing
    deeply and you see
Yourself

On the end of a pier
Stretching out into the water
Of a blue, blue lake
Roll the big rock that is on the end of the pier
Into the water and hear the splash
And watch the big ripples go out in circles.
In waves
From the hole in the water the rock made
For just a moment.
Now take a stone and heave it into the water
And watch the ripples, the circle of ripples
    ring out
And out from where the stone hit
Now throw some pebbles into the water and
Watch the many small ripples
The many, many ripples in the water go
    circling out
And now throw a handful of sand into
    the water
And see the hundreds of little ripples
    sprinkling the water
And throw another handful of sand and see
    some more.
But now, you are pushing your way through
    a black velvet curtain
Into a black, black room
You are looking for a black cat
There are black velvet curtains on the windows
Of this black room

And the floor is black plush
And the walls are black too
And the ceiling is panelled in black
    panelled wood
You are still looking for the black cat
And there it is on the keys of the black piano
    in the black room
And the keys are all black.
And it is there the black cat lies. Black on
    black, on black,
On black
It lies there purring.
Now open your eyes

There

A Catholic Shredding
in Beverly Hills

Nobody showed up for 8:00 mass this Sunday
Well not quite nobody
We like to delegate anybody with a coat on
To take the gifts up
Finally a black couple shows up nicely dressed
They are pressed into service
I sit alone at the back of the church
As the sermon starts
A nondescript figure in a brown suit
Walks in and stands behind me
A shopping bag in his hand
I sit there uneasily as he is standing by
The poor box and there have been thefts
I hear a rustling and I stand up
To check him out as he slowly tears the
Sunday "Tidings" newspaper in half and
Drops it on the floor
With a look at the priest in the pulpit
I start toward him and he leaves
The way he came in
I pick up the torn newspaper
And walk out after him
He is now climbing up the bank outside
The church and hanging the shopping bag
Which is full of "Tidings"
On the outstretched hands of the statue

Of the good shepherd
I say "get away from there, get"
And point down the street
He scurries away in the direction of
All Saints Episcopal and the
      Presbyterian Church
An ecumenical end to this story

Chauvinists Are Heir Born

I hate Hollywood kiss and tell books
      and stories
As much as anyone
But this brief tale is just
Bizarre enough to be told
It was just after World War II
And there was a photography fad
Involving a camera that took three dimensional
Pictures—stereoscopic
There was a large camera club with Harold Lloyd
      as president
That had monthly contests for best stereoscopic
Picture. I had never hoped to win until I met
One day with Tyrone Power.
We had both been in the Marine Corps
He as a pilot and me as an
Air controller

Ty knows a man with
A collection of airplanes he uses
To develop air inventions to improve the
      quality of flying
Since we are all interested in
      aerial photography
We hire two models to pose in the nude while
We fly over Los Angeles in a DC-3
We take off (so to speak) at 10:00 A.M. and
Orbit the Los Angeles area for two hours

We take lots of shots—the best is of Ty and a
    naked girl
In the cock pit with the Los Angeles skyline
    in the background
The girls of course are the only naked
    bodies aloft
And being professionals seem not a
    bit perturbed
Our amateurism is betrayed in the pictures
    we take

There are beads of perspiration standing out
In 3-D for all to see
Only on Ty and me of course
The shots turn out perfectly
But I don't think there are any extant
Our wives burnt them all
Strangely enough Ty's wife is the only one
    that is mad
My wife is happy that I spent the day
With Tyrone Power

We didn't win the contest
But to this day I watch the sky
Over Los Angeles and speculate
"What's in those airplanes?"
Women are funny

A Further Tyrone Power Chronicle

My friend said
"Ty Power always seemed a superficial actor
Till I saw him in Don Juan in Hell
He moved me
What was it with him?"

"He was ambivalent" I said
"Even about himself
He learned to piece himself out"
Twentieth Century worked him 24 hours a day
As an actor in one picture after another
And at night—as what?
The studio sent him out to be
Seen with a starlet every night
Twentieth had 10 male stars and
10 female stars
They tried to cross breed them socially
Ty, Cesar Romero, Don Ameche, etc
And Linda Darnell, Gene Tierney, etc
They got as many different duets
Out of those 20 as mathematics would allow
Is it any wonder
Ty seemed ambivalent
Just how ambivalent this true story will testify

One christmas eve he put on the classic red suit
And made up as Santa Claus and came to

Mandeville Canyon and knocked on our
      kitchen door,
A bag of toys on his back
Our black cook Becky opened the door
"An whom shall I say is callin?"
She said

Computer

The woman who comes every week
To help me with my computer
Says
Typing my stuff is
Affecting her lifestyle.
On her way to work every day
She sees a woman in weird clothes on Wilshire
With four parrots on each shoulder.
It's taking her a month of seeing her every day
To figure out the woman has clipped their tails
And they're stuck at home there.
This week, this day she sees the
Woman in a drug store in Westwood.
The birds aren't on her shoulder
She feels an impulse to say something—
Something to this poor, sad, weird,
        lonely woman
"Hello" she says "Where are your birds?"
The woman's scream almost knocks her down
"Who the fuck are you?"

How to Last in Show Business

When Ingrid Bergman told Alfred Hitchcock
A scene was difficult for her to act naturally
He told her, "fake it"
She said it was the best advice she ever got
He told me in "Shadow of a Doubt"
When I asked him how to play a scene
"Don't act"
"Let the camera do the work"
But if anyone should ask me
How to succeed in acting (which they haven't)
I would answer "just keep working"
But just as important is to keep eating
Food glorious food. An army moves on
        its stomach
So does an actor
When I was sharing a cheap apartment
In graduate school at Iowa
We each had to cook one dinner a week
I always did macaroni and cheese
I waited tables at the Kappa house
So the rest of my food was free
But it was food that got me through school
Starting in New York my first two years
Were feast or famine
My good months (I was working in
        radio) waiting
For that big break in the theatre
Which was waiting in the wings

I lived in the big room in a rooming house
And ate in the Automat or Nedick's
In poor months I lived in the small room
And lived for weeks on a gallon tin of
    peanut butter
And raw onions and whole wheat bread
Nutritionally it was perfect
The onions gave me vitamin C
The peanut butter vitamin B
The whole wheat bread E
The onions took the stickiness out of the
    peanut butter
The peanut butter sweetened the taste of
    the onion
As my career progressed and waned to
    movies overseas
Food, particularly cheese, helped me in times
Of crisis. Once I had to take the polar flight
From London to Copenhagen to L.A.
And go to work when I got off the plane—
A good thirty hours of travel time
And the plane was practically full
I came on board carrying a dozen small wheels
Of chèvre (that delicious goat cheese)
And a large wheel of Brie
The flight was booked solid but for one
    extra seat
My aromatic aura was enough
No one would come near me

So I stretched out on two seats
And slept well most of the trip
Food is glorious in many ways
The tragedy is that now I can afford it
I can't afford it
I have to diet
"Il faut souffrir pour etre belle"
If you're too fat you don't get the job
And besides
The wardrobe won't fit.

I Dress on the Left

"The Emperor's Clothes" was always
My favorite children's story
And clothes make the man the first slogan
I learned wrong
Because my mother kept this one of her boys
In knee pants or knickers
Longer than my age required or I demanded
Long pants were a badge of non-sissyhood that
Seemed when I got them long overdue
Taking them off became another signal
        of manhood
But that's another story

My first years as an actor I was a clothes horse
Wardrobe was deductible and since
        one shoulder
Was lower than another I couldn't wear
Clothes off the rack and got a good tailor
The tailor was expensive
Padded shoulders and lots of pockets were
        his specialty
He also did clothes for the mob:
Bugsy Siegel, Jack Dragna, etc.—suits with slits
And pockets for all kinds of weapons—
You name it. They were buried in his clothes
So yes, there are pockets in shrouds.

But now even dress extras can't
Deduct their wardrobe, which perhaps is
    one reason
Drawing room comedy died. The studios
Can't get the extras for banquet
And nightclub scenes
The tone of the cinema has faltered
And coarsened since my day.

Weatherstrips beat flap the wind
Machine break gas cold beer
Sign time up high as wave the flag
The clutch outstrips the gear
Hearts enroll in discipline
For amber staves of grain
Schlock me not nor spare the rod
Though gay the fruit is plain
His majesty is naked sure
No man of cloth is he
No cover up he deigns as sure as rains
    in Spain

Aquarius, Aquarius
I dread discharge at sea
And dress each dead and dying hood
From *T* to *T* to *T*

Maggie

She went with January
A Schnauzer of, if any determination
Irish in quality

It came to me to put her down
And as we entered the vet's
With her in hand
Three women sit there
With their pets; Corgi, Wolfhound,
    German Shepherd
They ask "why are you here?"
"To put her away", I say
And all three ladies burst into tears
I tell them four weeping women is three
    too many
And two leave the place
We wait for the doctor
He comes
"You've decided then", he says

Maggie, Her mistress and I
Enter the cold inner room—then
I am left with Maggie, Doctor and assistant
She makes one small lunge
To see where her mistress
Has gone
Then settles down
In my arms

The Doctor puts the needle in
A little light goes out in her eyes
And she goes too

Why are
The owners' phones always out of order
When a lost dog strays to my doorstep

Never give an animal
Too much of your love

We don't mourn a lover's death as much

First Will and Testament

There's nothing left to give you dear
The best is what I took
I begrudge it, it's the best of me
I swear it by the book
But it's just what you lack my dear
Because you gave it me before
I give it to you back my dear
I cannot give you more
So take it lest I change my mind
Before I weep and moan
I give you time yes time my dear
The time to be alone

If You Goof, Don't Bleed

World War II has just ended
But lots of big corporations in America
and England
Can't get their money out of other countries,
Shell Oil alone must have a billion tied up
in Spain
Which needs every dollar and pound to stay
even pretend solvent.

So I'm in Spain and Malaga with
Maureen O'Hara
Doing a movie for a British company
And an American producer and director
To get somebody's money out of the country
In the form of film

The producer's wife has brought in trunks of
Her old clothes for wardrobe for the extras
Most of whom are prostitutes
A regiment of Franco's army is being used
tomorrow as extras
They are being paid in wine
A bottle per man per day

The first scene is in the brothel
I'm tied to a pillar
And hit by the heavy

The heavy is an Englishman
Who's been brought along
From England as a stunt man. This is no
American stunt man who knows his business.
I try to tell him how to throw a roundhouse
Right hook aiming just short of my face—but to
Follow through and that I will take it
And above all not to be afraid of hitting me
Not to pull his punch. Of course
He is afraid. He pulls his punch.
He hits me right in the nose
"Cut" says the director, it's no good
You look as though you're afraid to hit him."
"I am" says the stunt man
"Well," the director says, "We'll try it again."
We do another take and he hits me again
Now my nose won't stop bleeding—
So the director puts a bullet proof vest on me
And shoots me
With blanks of course, I can actually feel
The blanks because I'm sensitive by now and
They are full load blanks at close
        range—which I have a
Healthy respect for since I've just finished a
Western where the villain shot himself in his
Private parts when his gun got caught in
        his holster
As he tried a fast draw.

At the end of the day I drive back to the
Hotel from the bordello with the whores
They precede me off the bus
The Spanish assistant who is their pimp
Gives the last girl a kick in the behind
To hurry her on her way.
I'm following him so I take one giant step to
    the rear and
Kick him in the ass
It's the end of an imperfect day.

"Just Let Us Make One Diagnosis We'll Know Vas Los Is"—Ira Gershwin

We have enough to do just staying
Alive and keeping out of the way of trucks
It's not bad enough as a human being having
An identity crisis—being an actor compounds it
George M. Cohan said "I don't care what
    they say
About me as long as they spell my name right."
Which is what Orville and Wilbur didn't say
But when the Boston Herald did a piece
A full column
Of misspellings of my name they misspelled
It in the lead

Mark Rothko suffered an identity crisis all
    his life
And at a party given for him when he was well
Established as a painter he ran out the door
Yelling at the hostess "you don't know who
    I am"
"You don't know who I am"
I gave a Japanese friend a book of his work
At Christmas
She wrote me "If you didn't send me this
Art book I'll never know
Who is Mark Rothko?"

As an actor I am equally pathetic
I delight in the mention of my name
Every day on the soap opera I do
And supreme bliss! My name was seventeen
    down in
Sunday's crossword puzzle and more people
Have mentioned that than have ever
    commented
On my acting or anything I've ever written
    or done
Dale Carnegie says "The sweetest sound
In all the world is the sound of your own name."

A rose by any other book
Lines round the clock and tackles back
    so neatly
Lime lightly pinks my look
Blush blooms by face in focus but succinctly

Is there a catch within the dream?
As rock rose the boat completely
Upwind of time we hear God's scream
"You buy the farm too cheaply."

The Law

Why everyone is surprised by the Beverly
    Hills Police
Overreacting on Rodeo Drive at Van Cleef
    and Arpels
Puzzles me
When my oldest boy Steve was ten he stole
Three goldfish from the Beverly Hills Park Pond
On Sunset Boulevard

I told him to return them

The police caught him putting them back
And two squad cars picked him up
And took him to jail
I had to go downtown
To get him out. They'd locked him up

It was a traumatic experience

He grew up to become
A Beverly Hills lawyer

Nobody Ever Said it Was Easy Being a Woman

Nobody ever said it was easy being a woman
One of our Ministers of the Eucharist is
And she says she had a hard time her first
Visit to give Communion

The sick old lady watched her as she said

The opening prayers of the ritual
And

When she put the host in the old lady's
    mouth
The old lady bit her finger

The Minister of the Eucharist
Had no response she could think of
She just went out and had a
Face lift

Oh For My Salad Days When I Was Green in Judgment

And wasn't I the good boy though
There I am on location at the Salton Sea
My wife, pregnant back in Los Angeles
And a group of us go into Juarez
To get loaded and visit a whore house
That is famous in the movie business

We're drinking Tequila and Bourbon and
      Southern Comfort
After turning down two wrong streets
We find it and instead of shaking hands
A young whore in the reception line
Avoids my outstretched hand
And shakes me between the legs
Everyone signs the house bible
Which has signatures of old stars
From Paramount and 20th for the last 40 years

And while my buddies have cosas sexuales
I sip my Southern Comfort on the piano bench
With the manager
And help him sweep out the living room
Until everyone is through

The next day I'm the only one with
A bad cold, a terrible hangover and a phone call
From a wife who doesn't believe this story

And another time
There I am on location in Africa
Just being ten thousand miles from home
In Africa isn't being away
Or alone for that matter

Last night in Nairobi the leopard tamer
      knocked
On my hotel door at midnight and wanted to
      come in
For a drink. For some reason I said no.
Today I see why. She had dated the
      assistant director
The night before and the company doctor
Is changing bandages today
On the scratches on his back.

So virtue is finally its own reward—but
      not really.
When I come home stateside when the
      picture is ended
My wife has cleaned my library
And thrown out all the dust wrappers on my
      first editions.

Joe, my barber, has his own philosophy
"All women are just con artists
From another country."

Orville

Just because he has an electric wheelchair
And I don't. He thinks he can talk to me
All night.
He can really tie up a telephone line

Sure the insertable toilet seat has screws
That cut his ass. Sure the tires get scraped
And his heels burn when he goes up ramps.
And the battery runs down when he goes from
Cahuenga to Laurel Canyon and back

But can't he talk about something beside
His electric wheelchair
There are more important things in life

To me

At least.

A Papal Visit

I am Pope
I pause while the procession forms
Behind me
My body is arched
Like a bow ready to
Loose an arrow
It is bent
From the assassin's bullets
My chest sewed to my stomach
To hold in my intestines

I am an actor in the wings
Waiting my cue
The crowd sees me—there is a roar
The flicker of a smile comes to my face
They like me

As quickly—the smile goes
I come to myself, to God
And I collect myself

Quicker than I smiled
I am within myself again
Gathering everyone around me
Into the place within me

I am Pope.

Parable

The first picture I made at Paramount
After the war was with Fred MacMurray
The first movie movie I'd made when I'd
Come out from New York four years before
Was with Fred MacMurray
I hero worshipped him
He was a star
But he'd remained unsnobbish
A human being
And one thing he said I'll never forget
"Never stay for the wrap party
After the picture"

Why not? I said and stayed
The first drink some big hulk of a grip
Comes over and tells me
What a great guy I am
To work with
The second drink
He begins hitting me on the
Shoulder—half joking—half serious
Third drink
He calls me a stuck up actor bastard

The exit is hard to find
The assistant wardrobe lady

Gets me out of there
Before I lose my skin

That's why you don't stay
For the wrap party

Resentment

Yesterday the bastard was leaving the shop
To go to the track
After I give him his haircut
And I give him twenty to lay on Lumbar
In the first
Well it wins and pays four thousand

He comes in this morning
And tells me he didn't get
To the window in time to place my bet

But not to worry Joe he says
I had your twenty on Primrose in the third
And she paid two sixty. Here it is

Well I throw the two sixty back
In his face and says give
Me my four thousand or else.
And do you know what he says?
He says do you want a hole in the head
Well I call the police
But not until I tell him what I think of him

I'll never let him forget it

And

I

Won't

Resurgence

I want to start again
I want to run past the cinder rocks
Walk the dark path through them to
    school again
And swing up the long swing when I push
My brothers swinging till I hope they would
And then hoped they wouldn't fall

And skate again
And feel my body good
Bumping against other bodies feeling
    leaning against
Then skate away stronger and faster
With a stick in my hand to hit them
Armed on ice
So strong from the skates
I don't take them off to drive
The car downtown and pick up Mother
At the Doctor's and a car slides into me
On Jackson Street right where
My dog died once
And I get out to stand
With the other driver on the icy road
Without my stick but still with my skates on
Or
Lie on my stomach till it aches
On the end of the pier staring

Into Lake Carlos I'd skip stones on
Staring at the yellow specks of pollen
Going down in the green green water
Till I couldn't see them anymore
And then be pulled behind a
Motor boat and the water rushing
Between my legs and then another ache
And then release
And I let my hands go off the rope
And I float on my back for a minute
Till they yell at me to get
Back in the boat and then leave me to
Swim ashore all by myself
At last to start again

Round and Round She Goes and Where She Stops Nobody Knows or The Price of Integrity Is Eternal Vigilance

We are all fatally flawed
Original sin I must believe in
As an actor I rejoice
But as a human being
I wince.

In my early days as a Hollywood actor
I am elected to the Screen Actors Guild
I watch Gene Kelly leap from the stage
To soothe Frank Sinatra
During a strike meeting
Now I sit on the stage
A newly installed Guild Board Member
My name is announced
I glow
Leon Ames turns to me
And says
They're not cheering you
Personally
It's because you're on the board
I remember this delight in power
When I have to build a character to play
But it's too bad I have it
When you get to be my age

There isn't much of your interior territory
You haven't explored
There are few trips you can take
Without stumbling over a familiar landmark
Oops
There you are again.

Was I a sultan in some past life
Revelling in the possession of houris
In my harem
It resurfaces today.

I am at a poetry reading
There is only a token
Presence of men
So many females
So much to do

When the reading is over
I obsessively
"Work the house"
I shake hands
I kiss everybody
I even rudely interrupt
A conversation
My poetry teacher is having
With two smouldering senoritas
From Buenos Aires

I show off my basic pedestrian
Spanish to flirt with them
I take a giant step
Toward creating an enemy
The teacher catches me at it
And I make an embarrassed exit
Leaving my glasses on the premises
Which is literally miles from home and
Loses me a day in the retrieval.

Once there was a chorus boy in a musical
The leading man shows up drunk one night
The stage manager taps the chorus boy on
      the shoulder
"You're on" he says and the chorus boy
      becomes a star
He also becomes a shit
Years later he is on his uppers
He's lost his fame
He's a chorus boy again
And one day—you guessed it—
He's sitting in the chorus boys dressing room
The stage manager comes in
Taps him on the shoulder
"You're on" he says.

I turn to the guy
Next to me in the dressing room
"Here comes that old shitty feeling"

I say
Well "merde" he says
Well "merde" I say
"I'm on." "I'm on again."

Show Business

Just as my peers do
I spend long days and long dreams
To hear these words

"Would you look over here"
"Could I have your autograph for my mother"
"For my daughter"
"For my friend"
"Make it out to Jane"

"I'm your biggest fan"
"I never miss anything you do"
"Who are you anyway?"
"Come on you're somebody, you must have
    a name"
"Aren't you Wendell Corey?"
"Your daughter is good. I can see where all
    your talent's gone"

"Sign my hat"
"Sign my bra"
"Sign my arm"
"Sign this check"

"Oh, leave him alone. He's nobody"

And now we play out our lives giving
Testimonial dinners
And awards to each other
If you live to be old enough
You can write your own notices

To Denise Levertov

It's spring cleaning
People are mating
Going on diets. Forgetting
Their morning prayers.

And I tell
The poet
I know a
Secret of life

She has told
In one sudden
Line of poetry
Her poetry
And I have read it

But I tell her
Where and when she got
The idea of it
The sense of it

There is a
Flash of appreciation
In her eyes
So I tell her
The secret

And she says
But no
That's not it
At all

You see

Two Dreams

I am in my garage unloading my car
I have left the door open to my house
A strange car drives up and a man gets out
And walks to my front door
I call to him. He doesn't turn or
      acknowledge me
I call his name and he turns to me for
Just an instant and says "You shouldn't have
      done that"
And walks into my house
The door closes after him
I know the man

I have started to sew—no to weave
A piece of cloth. But the yarn is a terrible
Indescribable color. It is a cloth I can't
Stop weaving. The yarn's color is making
      me sick
And afraid, yet I keep weaving, weaving. I can't
Change the yarn. I can't stop weaving.

(Untitled)

Can't we tell the truth or write it down
Scratch out the itch, suck out the suet
The burning molten marrow of our bones
And bare it seared white and black in
Ebony brilliance on blank pages—we are but
Greedy jays on patios
Dirt grey gulls on oil soaked beaches
Without stark honesty of
Black whores in white dresses
Clustered on corners of Sunset Boulevard
At 5:00 A.M. Daylight Saving Time
Trying for one last trick
Before sun's glacial glare or
Prowling black and whites turn them in
For pandering
To clucking prudes who put them there

Today's Visit to the Valley

Does it begin with weasel words?
"I didn't lie.
I made a pious deceit"
"No foundation down the line"
As he seated us
The maitre'de said "My ex-wife will be
Your waitress"
Clouds never part
"You forgot these magnetic paper clips
I wanted" I told the store clerk
"They're only three bucks, forget it.
I screwed up," she said, tossing them in
        my bag.
Life becomes more Bel Canto every day
One long vowel
Or did it begin with the pill
Erasing the word elopement

Evasion and desertion went public
Long ago
"I'm always home to you," I tell him
Sure, I'll answer his telephone calls
But that's all
And as for my secret life
Two nights a month is not quite enough to do—
I'm writing a book
I'll have you know I won't give anything away

Certainly not myself
When did it begin
Did it begin at all

(Untitled)

Every time I sit down to
Write I try to think
What I am going to write about
And nothing comes

But just watch
It'll be like the phone
Rings just when I go to the bathroom
Or leave the house and lock the door
      behind me

You watch
I'll get the idea for something
Illuminating and show stopping

But I'll be asleep and dreaming
An actor's dream
And forget my lines

So thank God I am
Awake

At least

I'm listening

(Untitled)

For a year now
I've tried to find the words
I've tried to find a way to tell you
Without hurting you

Yet today you thanked
Me for some small courtesy on the telephone
How you hurt me
When you said I was your friend

(Untitled)

There is a story that is told by actors since
There was a Hollywood and there was an
    East Coast
Two actors leave the Middle West to find fame
And fortune
One goes to Hollywood and one to New York
Neither one after ten years is working
    very much
In search of greener fields one
Gets on a plane and flies east
One gets on a plane and flies west
As they pass they yell to each other
Go back! Go back!

I'm trying to go back today
But back somewhere else
Back to the Middle West
Today I'm trying to write a poem
Of meanness and hate of revenge and despair
I'm digging tunnels to tunnels of resentment
And cravings and fears in my past
It ain't easy
Because
It is today and I have hope

But you can go home again if you try
There are ways

I am a child again at the boat club
In Sioux City. A boy of nine
I stand on the bank of the river and watch
A man tumble from his boat into the
        muddy water
I run for help but
No one comes. No one ever comes.

I dream of that man to this day
But even in my dreams I never find his body
In the muddy water that rushes past
And in my dream
Sometimes I'm in the water searching for
        him groping
And sometimes in my dreams I'm that man
        in the
Water and I know no one will ever find me
That's the way it is with me—the boy lost on
        the bank
The man lost in the water
I am both
Or

I am a boy again on Jackson Street in Sioux
        City
A boy of ten
I watch the car hit my dog
I run to the dog and yell at
The car which speeds on its way

I yell for someone to help me
Someone to help my dog
But no one helps me
No one comes
He dies there as I hold him
I dream this dream to this day too
Sometimes I'm the boy and sometimes I'm
    the dog
And sometimes I am both

This week my daughter
Is beginning to come out of her madness
She can take the bus herself now
And no longer cuts her wrists
Today she said "People aren't really
    marionettes, are they
They're really real people aren't they?"
I tell her yes, Lisa, yes they're really real people

Yesterday my daughter came late to therapy
Class and gave a wild cockamamie excuse
The doctor said "You're lying aren't you Lisa"
My daughter said "Well what do you know
I could have sworn I was telling the truth"

What Have You Got That Says You're Next?

When Leland Hickman asked me why did I
    go to the seminar with the
Poets
Why did I feel I had to answer "Maybe
    something will rub off on me"
He was there himself the next seminar at
    my house
And left early, disappointed—and didn't even
    look at me

Last night my brother is driving four of us to
    an AA meeting
And can't find the address
He says he's sure it's the next block and I
    agree with him
We get to the next block and it's not the
    address at all
"My brother is wrong" he says

Yesterday the girl behind the counter says
    "Who's next"
"I am" the man next to me says
"My number is 86" I say "What have you got
    that says you're next"
"I say so" the man says
In Guitry's "Pearls of the Crown"

The leader of the thieves divides the
        seven pearls
"Two for you, two for you, and three for me"
"How come" the other two thieves say
"Because I am the leader" he says
"How come you're the leader" they say
"Because two for you, two for you
And three for me"

And I have just advised my daughter
Not to resent the critic who
Gave her the rotten notice
But to pray for him

"Why does he go around talking like that"
Old Joe says at the AA meeting last night
"Have you ever met this guy calls himself
        Captain Serenity?
"What does he mean Captain Serenity?
His fucking name's Fred

Who Was That Masked Man?

You can go years
Without realizing
Other people know things
About you
That you don't

You could walk down
The street and
Pass yourself
Without knowing who
It was
You passed

It's hard enough
To catch up
With yourself
And then it doesn't
Do you any good
Because you don't know
Who it is
You've caught up with

The only one
Who really knows
Is the girl
The girl
You first danced with

Keep dancing with me, girl
Don't stop
Please don't stop
If you do
I can't stand
I fall down
I tip over.

What We Have Here Is a Failure to Communicate

I don't know the answer to your question
I guess "Be prepared" would be the best
In the Second World War I remember going
        ashore on a Pacific Island
To the south of Espiritu Santo in a boat
We had cadged from the Navy Pool for the day
It was early in the war—the Japanese still
        held Bougainville
But we had the day off. We walked ashore,
        two off duty Marine Officers
And introduced ourselves to the island
        residents—a Scot missionary couple
Who gave us tea and gingerale and invited us to
Play tennis on their immaculately kept lawn
        tennis court
The net was taut, the lines were chalked
        clean white
On the clipped green grass court
"Why," we asked them "Do you keep a court
        on this island
In the midst of the Pacific. Why do you
        keep it?"
"Are you that rabid tennis enthusiasts?"
"No," they said, "We don't play. But someone
        might drop in."

Being lucky is important, but being ready for
      good luck
Is more important
The night the magician picked me from the
      audience of excited little boys
To draw the rabbit out of the hat and let me
      keep it
I didn't
Because Mother wouldn't let me
We had to leave town the next day on
      vacation and rabbits
Presumably don't travel
And this week when my nephew Matthew
      told his stepmother
He was going to catch a fly ball at the Dodger
      game on his birthday
A foul fly ball hit him in the mouth and
      knocked loose
All his lower teeth. The actual stitches on the
      ball were imbedded
In his gums.

The most interesting thing that ever
      happened to my mouth
Was receiving a radio program on two fillings
      in my teeth
Between Roxbury and Mapleton on
      Sunset—Where I was driving that is

I had just been to the dentist and the new
    platinum filling
And the old silver made a perfect crystal set
(Given the acid condition of my stomach
    and mouth)
Reception was passable but there was too
    much interference
From the CB's that were in vogue that year.
This was no ham radio operator I was
    receiving but KFAC
A classical music station.
Nowadays I don't get a clear signal in
    my house
I live in a canyon.

The reception is so bad I watch little TV and
    listen to little radio.
I read.
Communication has been constantly difficult
    for me
The one movie I made in Africa the majority
    of my scenes involved
Different tribes in Kenya—The Turkhana,
    Bantu, Masai and
Kikuyu so
I ad libbed most of the picture in what is the
    lingua franca
Of all Africa—Swahili. The picture never quite
    came off

Because when I had to dub a major part of
        the movie back in England
I hadn't taken notes and had to guess at the
        words to match my mouth.

Is it any wonder the words of signature on
        the soap opera I have done
For twenty-three years are misunderstood. I
        say "this is Macdonald Carey."
At the beginning and end of each show five
        times a week
Two people as distant and disparate as a
        housewife in Ohio
And an air stewardess from Memphis,
        Tennessee have written me
The identical story. Their eight-year old boys
        have each
At one time or another come to them and
        said, "It's 12 o'clock Mommy,
Time to turn on the TV. Time to listen to 'My
        dumb old carrot.'
Of course that's me
Macdonald Carey.